"Honor Thy Mother": Part 2

A Prophetic Intercession of Comfort & Healing: Honoring Mother's Overcoming Grief with The Power of Building Their Loved One's Legacy and Amplifying their Own Voices with Encouraging Testimonies, Prayer & Advocacy!

Visionary Author. Rev. S. Sewell
Contributing Author's: Gwendolyn Stewart, Rochica McBryde, Linda Mercer, Min.Wendi Milbourne, Min. Zinya Smith, and India Jiminez.

Copyright © 2023 S.Sewell, All rights reserved; Co-Author's are authorized to use reproduce their own stories, for transformative use.

TABLE OF CONTENTS

CHAPTER 1
A Mother's Heart to Heart & Intercession
Honoree: Mrs. Gwendolyn Stewart   pg. 3-17

CHAPTER 2
A Mother's Heart to Heart Commitment to Building Her Son's Legacy
Honoree: Ms. Rochica Mcbryde   pg. 18-21

CHAPTER 3
The Healing Power of Prayer: The Intercession by. Rev. Sewell
                                          pg. 22-27

CHAPTER 4
A Mother's Heart to Heart Commitment to Amplifying Her Voice to Encourage Christian Mothers
                                          pg. 28-29

CHAPTER 5
A Mother's Heart to Heart Commitment to Self-Love, Self-Care, and Women's Empowerment! Honoree: India Jiminez
                                          pg.30-31

CHAPTER 6
An Intercessory Prayer For All Mother's
Honoree: Min. Wendi Milbourne   pg.32-36

CHAPTER 7
An Intercessory Prayer For Healing and Restoration of Family
Honoree: Min. Zinya Gray   pg.37-39

CHAPTER 8
Healing from Injustice Trauma with the Power of Forgiveness, Worship and Advocacy!   pg. 40-50

CHAPTER 1

A Mother's Heart to Heart & Intercession

Honoree: Mrs. Gwendolyn Stewart

A Mother's Heart to Heart & Intercession Honoree: Mrs. Gwendolyn Stewart

It is with a humble and grateful heart that I share our story and our testimony of how God brought us through. On August 10, 1986, the Lord blessed us with a beautiful 2 pound 10 ounce baby girl, Jaclyn Laniece Wright. She was a fighter. So much so even the doctors and nurses in the neonatal care unit were impressed with her tenacity, strength, and determination to live. She was very sassy yet classy at the same time with a hint of fire by the time she started to walk. She captivated anyone that came into her presence.

As I watched her grow, she could command any room she entered. I believe that if God would have allowed her to live to adulthood she would have become the hairdresser she desired to become. Jackie was very bold, a wonderful listener, an encourager and motivator. In the seven years that she lived, she grew to be one of the most inspirational little people in my life although to me she only lived a short life but to God she lived a full life. God knew her best and the number of years she was to be in our lives; 7 years, the number of completion.

In 1993, on February 6th, I remember receiving a phone call from her older cousin that informed me that my Jackie, as she was affectionately known to us; had been hit in the head with a brick. Though alarming it was; the words that followed caused me to drop to my knees.

I felt like I was suffocating. I felt my heart stop beating and I couldn't catch my breath. That day the life of my daughter, Jaclyn Wright transitioned to be with the Lord and my most inspirational and encouraging (gift?) was no longer with us. One might say, "How do you know she's with the Lord?" On September 2, 1992, at the tender age of 7, Jaclyn "Jackie" Wright accepted and received Jesus Christ as her Lord and Savior.

Now here is where I must be very transparent with everyone. At this time my prayer life wasn't very grounded, and I didn't know how to call on the Father in prayer for strength to get through this process. I was hurt, I was angry; I was mad, and I was shaken. Our world had been turned upside down by the senseless act of someone that I let into my world and trusted with my kids. At that time in my mind I could only think of the scripture in Exodus 21:23-24.

Exodus 21:23-24 - New King James Version

23 But if any harm follows, then you shall give life for life, 24 eye for eye, tooth for tooth, hand for hand, foot for foot, 25 burn for burn, wound for wound, stripe for stripe.

During this season of my life I was seasoned enough in the Word of God to know what the Word said regarding vengeance; with that understanding I knew that if I tried to seek vengeance on my own that it would not turn out the way I wanted and the lives of my two sons would be left in the balance. Being reminded of yet another scripture in Romans 12:19-21;

"Dearly beloved, avenge not yourselves, but rather give place unto wrath: for it is written, Vengeance is mine; I will repay, saith the Lord. Therefore if thine enemy hunger, feed him; if he thirst, give him drink: for in so doing thou shalt heap coals of fire on his head. Be not overcome of evil, but overcome evil with good."

We must always be aware of what type of season we are in. How I handled that season of my life would determine my future and the future of my sons. This traumatic event not only affected me, it also affected their lives as well. It was during this time of our lives I learned that grief affects children in a totally different way than it affects adults. We want to believe that children are resilient and that they will bounce back with little to no recollection of what has happened. It is what I would call "Unrealistic thinking.

As a single mother raising two sons that had just seen their sister for the last time. having to explain to a 6 year old and an 11 year old that they would never see their sister again was the most difficult task I ever had to do. It was a very difficult time for each of us. My youngest became very challenged and had a hard time expressing his feelings; returning to school was very difficult for him and for him it was difficult to focus. I didn't learn until later that my oldest son was dealing with anger and that art was his outlet. Their grades suffered and needless to say we had to seek professional guidance for us all.

As a mother, I did not consider how this affected my sons or my daughter's father. In the greatness of the hurt I could only see this hurt as something I alone was enduring. I needed to be delivered from myself. I was so angry with her dad and her grandfather.

When I came to myself, I realized that this hurt was great for her dad and granddad I never considered that until several months into my grieving process as to how selfish my actions and feelings were. He nor I could see the threat. This was someone we trusted in our daughter's life.

What I learned is that the enemy did not and does not care who he uses to invade your life. In our case, the snake was within the inner circle of our family We did not even see it because I was so distracted by this woman's attitude regarding our ability to co-parent and remain friends. I did not see the threat, nor did I seek God for what I now know as his Gift of Discernment when I sensed there was something off in her spirit.

In the months that followed this tragic event I became overly protective and didn't want my sons visiting anyone overnight unless it was my immediate family only. I was very angry with her father for months. I didn't even consider the pain he was suffering because in my mind he brought this woman into our lives and did not pay attention to the signs that may have been present.

To be blatantly honest I was even mad with God. I could not understand how God could let something like this happen to a child but even more to my child.

I was serving him with all my heart and could not understand how this happened. I needed some serious intervention. I needed to be delivered from anger, bitterness and selfishness. I was acting as if I was the only person going through this pain. Then the Holy Spirit reminded me of Mary, the mother of Jesus who found favor with the Lord.

Honoring Mary, Mother of Jesus Christ As A Mother Who Shared In Christ's Sufferings And Grief: We Are Not Alone

Mary, served God well; so well that it was stated by the angel of the Lord, Gabriel in Luke 1:28

"And the angel came in unto her, and said, Hail, thou that art highly favored, the Lord is with thee: blessed art thou among women."

Mary gave birth to Jesus, God's one and only son, the Savior of the World. If you have never seen the movie "The Passion of the Christ" I highly recommend it. It provides a very good depiction of what Jesus Christ endured before and while he was going to the cross. It absolutely will help you understand what this mother had to endure as she stood by watching the Roman soldiers as they began to brutally whip her first born child mercilessly; whipping him 39 times for the sins we willingly committed.

Let me be blatantly honest; at the moment everything within me wanted to kill this person. She murdered my daughter. However, I was and continue to be encouraged when I imagine Mary; for the sake of the entire world, had to endure a greater pain so that the call and purpose that was on Jesus' life would be fulfilled.

Mary understood what Jesus' purpose and assignment was. Whether or not she knew the depth or severity of the process of what he would endure; God placed people in her path that would undergird her through the process. Did it make the process easier; well that's a question only Mary can answer when we get to heaven and ask her.

Just as Mary understood Jesus' purpose and assignment while here on earth, we have a purpose and an assignment and so do the children we are blessed to nurture in this world. Unless we understand that purpose and assignment is what we risk; thus, opening the door for the enemy to come in and derail, delay or even cause their purpose and assignment as well as our own, to be sabotaged because we allow someone in our environment or in our circle of influence to infiltrate the circle.

I can only imagine how helpless Mary felt even though she understood Jesus' purpose and assignment, as she looked on as her own flesh and blood was being brutally whipped before her eyes then nailed to a cross for the sins of the world, our sins. Please understand that by no means am I minimizing the pain we all have endured, are enduring and sometimes still feel over the transitioning of our loved ones by sickness or by someone else's actions.

    For us it has been 30 years since we had to endure this tragic event. Crying seemed like it would never end. I found myself in relationships to try to medicate the pain and drifted further away from God even though my family was praying for me. I just could not wrap my head around what had happened, especially during moments such as her birthday, Mother's Day, my birthday, and other special occasions but I have learned to lean more on Jesus in those moments when I become overwhelmed.

    During that season of our life, we had more saints of God praying for and with us that the weight of it all did not seem as heavy. It was that support system that brought me through in that season. If I can submit to you, I believe if it wasn't for my support system, professional support and most importantly my faith in God our lives would be totally different.

Having people to pray with you and for you will help with the process of the grief. Leaning on Jesus and the indwelling power of the Holy Spirit that lives within every believer will give us the strength to fight and get the victory that Jesus has promised us.

Can you imagine the grief and heartache Mary felt during that traumatic moment of her life? Can you imagine Joseph telling Mary she must move on with her life and stop grieving? Unless you have endured this type of pain, please I beg of you; do not tell someone how long they should grieve their loved one.

Grief does not come with an expiration date. It is a completely different monster. It must be handled properly, or it will take us into a place where the enemy will have his way with us. It may lead some to drink, some to dive deeper into lust, or some into or deeper into drugs No matter what your vice is, know that grief is a process that everyone that encounters the loss of a loved one has to go through on their own because it affects each person differently. Grieve because you must in order to overcome the pain of the loss but have a support system to help you through.

EMBRACING THE POWER OF PRAYER FOR COMFORT AND HEALING

As a mother, prayer has given me greater strength and it has helped me to realize that I can cast my cares on the Lord. I don't have to carry the weight of my troubles on my shoulders because Jesus paid the price to carry them on his shoulders. 1 Peter 5:7,**"casting all your care upon him; for he careth for you."**

MY PRAYER OF INTERCESSION: LORD INCREASE OUR STRENGTH

Prayer of Strength:

Ephesians 3:16 - 17 King James Version

16 That he would grant you, according to the riches of his glory, to be strengthened with might by his Spirit in the inner man; 17 That Christ may dwell in your hearts by faith; that ye, being rooted and grounded in love,

Father according to Ephesians 3:16-17; I pray above all else that you would grant "child's (rens) names" to be strengthened in their inner man by Your Spirit according to the riches of Your glory in Christ Jesus. Father, I pray that you would dwell in their hearts by faith and may they be rooted and grounded in Your love. In Jesus Mighty Name. Amen

5 NUGGETS FOR DEVELOPING A SPIRITUAL RELATIONSHIP WITH YOUR FAMILY , WHILE OVERCOMING GRIEF

- **Nugget #1: Engage in an open dialogue and not a monologue. Allow yourself to be vulnerable.**

- **Nugget #2: Be a GOOD LISTENER.**

- **Nugget #3: Think, process, then speak.**

- **Nugget #4: Do not be judgmental or critical of them, because they are hurting too.**

- **Nugget #5: Invite them to study the Bible with you by asking them what they would like to know about in the Bible then ask them their perspective, listen, then share yours.**

<u>A PRAYER TO HELP YOU OVERCOME GRIEF ON MOTHER'S DAY</u>

Psalm 30:5 For his anger endureth but for a moment; in his favour is life: weeping may endure for a night, but joy cometh in the morning. Revelation 21:4 Scripture tells us that God shall wipe away all the tears from our eyes; Deuteronomy 31:6 - Be strong and of good courage, fear not, nor be afraid of them: for the LORD thy God, he it is that doth go with thee; he will not fail thee, nor forsake thee.

May you find comfort during this special day. Your weeping may endure for a night but know this one thing according to Psalm 30:5, joy will come in the morning. In every memory that you reflect on, may you find strength. So be strong and of good courage, do not be afraid. May the joy of the Lord be your strength and know that God will turn it around for your good.

Gwendolyn Stewart's Dedication:

To My Family: Thank you for being the best support system a person could ever have. Because of you I was able to become the person that I am today.

Edward Hamilton: Domestic violence left a hole in your heart that you may believe can never be filled. God is a heart fixer and mind regulator. Forgive me for all the time that I spent being angry with you for the loss of our daughter. Thank you for blessing me with such an amazing little girl and for the years we had to pour into her life.

Chante' Simmons: Though the pain may never completely go away and when those moments arise of wanting to hug your son Levoy come, think of your proudest moment when he made you smile. May God continue to strengthen you and your family.

CHAPTER 2

A Mother's Heart to Heart Commitment to Building Her Son's Legacy

Honoree: Ms. Rochica Mcbryde

Mother's Heart to Heart Commitment to Building Her Son's Legacy
Honoree: Ms. Rochica Mcbryde

I am Rochica McBryde, CEO of Heavenlytaste By Chica. I started this business is April 1, 1999. I had a restaurant for 16 1/2 years located in Silver Springs, Md. After the Restaurant closed on April 2015, I decided to get a food truck and continued my business. I received my business License for my Food Truck on April 30, 2015.

In the midst of great success and blessings, tragedy struck; the worse thing that any Mother' could imagine, happen in my Life. I lost my son Gregory McBryde at the age of 21. He was a victim of murder and my life change; and my life took a complete U turn.

I went into a deep depression, but I knew my life couldn't stay there. My healing process has been so hard; but I knew that I had to get up out of depression. Building my Son's legacy was something that I knew that God wanted me to do.

In the midst of my own struggle and pain; I decided to start at support Group by faith, focusing on others who have also suffered a loss.

 I felt we could help each other by this support Group. I've met so many moms and families who understood my grief, and it is from the strength gathered from the support of others that I realized. The support group was the best thing I could have done.

The bible declares that "**He comforts us in all our affliction, so that we may be able to comfort those who are in any kind of affliction, through the comfort we ourselves receive from God**". 2 **Corinthians 1:4.** Each year I give back to grieving mothers by planning a Remembrance Brunch and Pre-Mother's every year; this bring a lot of peace to my heart by helping others.

Rochica's Dedication Heavenly Taste By Chica Catering Business and Our Hearts Have Wings Started in memory of my son, Gregory McBryde Aka OCG

CHAPTER 3

The Healing Power of Prayer: The Intercession

By. Rev. Sewell

A Prophetic Intercession of Comfort & Healing
Visionary Author. Rev. S. Sewell

1. Heavenly Father, we come to You today humbly seeking healing and deliverance. In our brokenness, we long for physical, emotional, and spiritual healing and relief. We place our faith in You, knowing that You have the power to do what is needed and make a way where there seems to be no way.

2. Your Word assures us that You are the Healer and that by Your stripes we are healed. As we bow before You, Lord, we thank You that Your Word is true. Your Word has given us the power to declare what You have promised over our lives and those of our loved ones.

3. So, today we come in faith asking for You to renew us, restore us, and grant us healing. Whether that is complete healing and deliverance, or healing for our journey, we ask for Your wisdom and peace to surround us in our journey.

4. God, we acknowledge that You are in control, and nothing is impossible with You. Thank You that You do not forget

us. Hear our pleas, our groaning and our cries. Comfort us as only You can. Strengthen our faith, help us to have an even deeper trust in You, and deliver us from all fears, anxieties, and sorrow.

5. Lord, we bring the burdens and pains of our hearts to You and ask that You wipe away our tears. Guide us and bring clarity in times of darkness and uncertainty. Give us strength, wisdom, and courage. Open paths for us and give us favor. Speak to our situation and fill us with Your healing power, love, and peace.

6. Lord, as we place our hope in You and accept the work of deliverance You are doing in us, we pray in the name of Jesus. Amen.

7. Heavenly Father, we thank you for the blessings you have given us, both tangible and intangible. We come before you with a prayer of peace and joy in our hearts. We pray for peace throughout our world. Grant us a peace that passes all understanding.

8. We also ask that you fill our lives with joy and love, Lord. Let our hearts overflow with gladness and contentment that come only from you. Give us peace in times of worry, courage in times of uncertainty, and faith in times of adversity.

9. We give you thanks, Lord, for all you have done for us. Through your mercy and grace, you have saved us. Bless us

and guide us every day so that we can be a beacon of hope to others. Help us to seek justice, show mercy, and share in your divine love for all of your people.

10. Grant us this peace and joy so that we may live in harmony, knowing that your loving arms embrace us and protect us always. Amen.

11. Lord Jesus, we come before You today in repentance and humility. We confess and lament our sins that have caused separation between You and us.

12. We thank You for Your love and mercy. Even when we fail, Your love and faithfulness remains steadfast.

13. We ask You to restore and redeem us. Wash us with the Blood of Your Son Jesus and heal our wounds.

14. Grant us Your mercy and restore us to the life we were called to live. May our hearts turn away from darkness and toward You, our Heavenly Father.

15. Strengthen us in our walk and guide our paths in the way You would have us go.

16. Grant us a humble and contrite heart, ready to receive Your grace and direction. Help us to obey Your commands and walk in Your love.

17. Almighty Father, we come to You in need of restoration and renewal for our minds and our lives. As we reflect on all of our failings, weaknesses, and limitations, we surrender all of these things to You, trusting in Your

limitless love, grace, and mercy.

18. We lift our eyes to You, trusting in Your goodness and power to sustain us, restore us, and empower us to become the people You intended us to be. Help us to resist temptation, temptation of power, lust, and the destruction of our spirit. Give us strength to turn away from that which seeks to destroy us and move us away from You.

19. Fill our hearts and minds with hope, peace, and contentment that only You can give. With You as our foundation, fill our lives with direction, purpose, and freedom, allowing us to serve You to our fullest potential.

20. Give us the knowledge and insight to realize what we truly need and desire, providing us with patience and humility to accept our imperfections, struggles, and brokenness. Let us use our struggles as fuel to move closer to You, our true refuge, sustainer, and protector.

21. Fill us with Your love, so that we can in turn, share it with those around us, our families, friends, neighbors, and even those we do not know. Help us to use this newfound wisdom and guidance to become closer to You, allowing our spiritual, physical, and mental well-being to be the product of the wonderful work You are doing within us.

22. We offer our prayers up to You with love, adoration, and faith, knowing You will bring us all the peace and strength we need to continue living in Your abundant grace. We

love and trust You, Lord. In Jesus name Amen.

23. Heavenly Father, we thank You for Your faithfulness and loving kindness. You have made us in Your image, with all our diverse gifts, strengths, and talents.

24. We come to You today in a spirit of prayerful gratitude, asking for peace and joy for each person, family, and community on this planet. Give us peace to face the darkness and struggles that come to our way and a joy to appreciate the beauty and grace of this world.

25. We know that in times of fear and uncertainty You provide hope and assurance, and in the presence of sorrow You can bring a well of comfort and healing.

26. Let us each live as a blessing to others in every way, providing compassion and solace as You would. Give us courage to speak out and to stand up for the marginalized and oppressed, and never let us forget those who are facing sorrow or illness.

27. God, You know all of our needs, so pour out Your peace and joy into our hearts and souls today. Fill us with the divine hope of Your Spirit and ignite our hearts with Your healing love, to light the way in dark places. Amen.

28. Lord, let Your name be glorified and praised by all who live and follow You. Amen.

CHAPTER 4

A Mother's Heart to Heart Commitment to Amplifying Her Voice to Encourage Christian Mothers

Honoree: Mrs. Linda Mercer

A Mother's Heart to Heart Commitment to Amplifying Her Voice to Encourage Christian Mothers

Honoree: Ms. Linda Mercer

I am getting ready to launch my heavenly creations, comfort services to help others cope with the loss of a love one.

Tips for the Christian Mother
Invest energy with the Lord consistently! For it is God, and God Alone Who will bring you through !

"Christianity isn't really for just one time each week; Christianity is for Every Day". I say this because to guarantee that we are a Christian is to say that we are a supporter of Christ. Whenever we say we love Jesus we should want to invest consistent time and worship in His presence consistently; because He is truly the God who heals and comforts all wounds.

CHAPTER 5

A Mother's Heart to Heart Commitment to Self-Love, Self-Care, and Women's Empowerment!

Honoree: India Jiminez

A Mother's Heart to Heart Commitment to Self-Love, Self-Care, and Women's Empowerment!
Honoree: Ms. India Jiminez

Author, India Jiminez is the mother to three amazing children and lover of self unapologetically. She is a Podcast founder and host of Not Just The Mamas 2.0 Experienced Edition coming soon to YouTube and will be available on all podcast platforms. She is experienced in areas of education, mental health and a dash of good ole living life with people in need of love without judgement. Bringing love, light and peace to others is what she lives for! Find yourself needing an escape from the challenges of life connect with her judgment free podcast. Not Just The Mamas 2.0 Experienced Edition coming soon to YouTube.

CHAPTER 6

An Intercessory Prayer For All Mother's

Honoree: Min. Wendi Milbourne

An Intercessory Prayer for All Mother's Honoree: Min. Wendi Milbourne

Let us look to the Lord, Father God in the matchless name of Jesus, I cry out to you lifting the children that are connected to anyone that hears this prayer. Lord God you have but loaned our children to us for a season, I believe in your word because you are a God that can not lie I give your words back to you. Isaiah 54:17 "No weapon that is formed against thee shall prosper and every tongue that shall rise against thee in judgment thou shalt condemn. This is the heritage of the servants of the Lord and the righteous is of me saint the Lord. " Your word is true and are a promise to those that that diligently seek you.

By the power of the Holy Spirit I cancel every assignment of the enemy that seek to steal, kill and destroy. I bleed the blood of Jesus over them. They shall live and not die. I declare the works of you God in their lives. They are forever and will be successful, they are prosperous, they have favor and abundance. I boldly declare it is done in the name of our savior Jesus the Christ

Lord God, you said in your word Acts 16:31 if we believe in the Lord Jesus that we would be saved. God you promised to save us and our entire household. Your word is a blueprint for our lives, help us to stand on your promises. Lord God and if you do these things I will be so careful to give your name all the praise, honor, and glory. So let the words of my mouth and the meditation of my heart be acceptable in thy sight oh Lord my strength and my redeemer in Jesus name. Amen

It is truly humbling, to be honored, as it reflects my spiritual growth and maturity another opportunity to share the goodness of the Lord on a larger platform. A portion of the prayer of Jabez says enlarge my territory being featured in this manner shows me once again God still hears and answers my prayers.

Mother's Day is hard for so many; I know you heart is heavy; I myself have been in this space of sadness. I admonish you to give all the hurt, pain, sorrow and sadness to the Lord.

Open your mouth cry out to Him, share your feelings hopes and dreams for He cares for you. Jesus is the answer give it all to Him and He will comfort your heart. He will strengthen and establish you. Lord God send your angel of comfort to give them hope in this difficult time. Cover them with your blanket of peace to soothe their broken heart.

Remember weeping endorses for a night but joy cometh in the morning. God understands your heartache and wants to heal you everywhere you hurt, let Him in. Although you may feel alone at this time God is with you always, He will never leave you nor forsake you. Isaiah 41:10 "So do not fear I am with you, do not be dismayed, for I am your God I will strengthen you and help you, I will uphold you with my righteous right hand.

Time heals all wounds, carry on your loved ones legacy remember the them in a positive way. Sooner than you may think you will be able to smile and laugh and make merry again in your loved ones honor.

Min. Milbourne's Dedication:

Dear Grandmother Sarah Johnson- Watts,

I am dedicating chapter to you because of your influence and example of never wavering faith in Christ Jesus has impacted my life, even though God took you when I was only 8 yrs old I will forever cherish those moments I'd stop by your house after school before going home to share with you first what new thing I had learned. Your warm smile and encouraging words are still with me.

CHAPTER 7

An Intercessory Prayer For Healing and Restoration of Family
Honoree: Min. Zinya Gray

An Intercessory Prayer for All Mother's Honoree: Min. Zinya Gray

Father God, in the name of Jesus, your word is alive and powerful; and you have given us a spirit of power, love, and a sound mind, discipline and self-control. You have qualified us as women of greatness, peculiar people.

We will honor you for healing our hearts, minds, and for indwelling in our lives. We will bless your name at all times, whether we are successful or are experiencing challenges in life. We honor and giving thanks to you for qualifying us to share the inheritance of Jesus Christ.

I pray to you Father God for giving us every blessing in heaven because we belong to you in Jesus name. Hallelujah! You have given us all we need for life and godliness through the knowledge of you. I rejoice in Jesus because you are stirring up the gifts in all of us. I pray for healing for us all. We will never feel abandonment because you promised to never leave, nor forsake us Lord. I pray that if your mother is alive, that the Lord will increase your relationship with spiritual success; and that if your Mother is resting in the presence of the Lord, that your will glean in on the happy memories of times shared with the expectation that you shall see your loved one again.

Father in the name of Jesus, I come before you with a word of prayer to strengthen my brothers and sisters with the power of intercession. There are many who have cried and could not dry their tears on their own and are standing in need of comfort. But with you Lord you have spoken a word unto them to dry their tears from disappointment, setbacks, loneliness, and a broken heart. Your holy word declares us in Psalms 30 verse 5, weeping may endure for a night, but joy will come in the morning.

Min. Gray's Dedication:

I dedicate this chapter to all of the women out there to my family and Friends because we all have a mother that we want to love some of us might not have a mother but there is someone out there who really loves you and wants to be there for you, to encourage you to help you, to support you and to pray with you.

CHAPTER 8

Healing from Injustice Trauma with the Power of Forgiveness, Worship and Advocacy!

Healing from Injustice Trauma with the Power of Forgiveness, Worship and Advocacy!

Visionary Author
Rev. Starsha Sewell

Injustice trauma is a deeply painful experience that can cause significant harm to an individual's mental, emotional, and spiritual well-being. However, forgiveness is a powerful tool that can help individuals heal from the wounds of injustice trauma.

In the Bible, Jesus teaches the importance of forgiveness and the need to love our enemies **(Matthew 5:44)**. By forgiving those who have wronged us, we are not only freeing ourselves from the burden of anger and bitterness but also acknowledging that justice is ultimately in the hands of God **(Romans 12:19)**. Forgiveness allows us to move forward and heal from the trauma of injustice, and ultimately, to live a life of freedom and joy **(Colossians 3:13).**

The concept of injustice trauma and how it affects individuals and communities. Injustice trauma is a pervasive issue that can have devastating effects on individuals and communities. The Bible recognizes the pain of injustice and the need for restoration and justice for those who have been wronged **(Isaiah 1:17)**. Injustice can cause feelings of anger, sadness, and despair, which can lead to long-term trauma. However, the Bible also offers hope for healing and restoration through forgiveness **(Ephesians 4:32)** and advocacy **(Micah 6:8).**

Recognizing the reality of injustice trauma and the power of forgiveness is the act of mind renewal that onsets healing and quality of life transformation; that is only available when we decide by faith that we are going to try for the sake of our own emotional well-being, but it is something that we can only do when we become "sick and tired of being, sick and tired" literally.

Many people find it challenging to forgive, because they think that God expects them to move on from their losses; However, in my own revelation; God revealed to me that when it comes to some issues forgiveness is not about "**Moving On**"; it was about me "**Moving Over**" to the other side of the matter, after the fact. God understands that we can't change some of the things that happened; but what He knows is that His promise to give us an abundant life is still available, and that all things can still work together for your good even if it hurts; but only if we let it. Jesus desires for us to be fruitful, and this work challenges Mother's who are overcoming grief in diverse capacities to understand their value as a Mother on the other side of unexpected evil. When Jesus 'friend Lazarus died, he groaned. He groaned so that you would understand that it is acceptable to groan, but on the other side of groaning Jesus took back His friend from the grave; and I commend and lift up the arms of every Mother in this book, who is fighting to take back their loved one's legacy with their own fruitfulness.

Forgiveness is your exit strategy that empowers you to fight back against the adversaries evil; because meditating on the evil of the adversary is what harms your life, your health, your strength, and allows the enemy to continue the warfare of destroying God's plan for your life.

Forgiveness is a supernatural way of escape to free yourself from the bondage that the enemy used against your quality of life. The Bible is full of examples of individuals who have used forgiveness as a tool for healing from injustice trauma.

Joseph forgave his brothers who sold him into slavery and wronged him greatly **(Genesis 50:15-21)**. Stephen, in the midst of being stoned to death, forgave those who were killing him **(Acts 7:60)**. Jesus himself forgave those who crucified him, saying *"Father, forgive them, for they know not what they do"* **(Luke**

23:34). These examples show the transformative power of forgiveness in the face of injustice trauma.

Practicing forgiveness is not always easy, but it is crucial for our spiritual and emotional well-being. The Bible offers practical steps for practicing forgiveness, including acknowledging our own faults **(Matthew 7:1-5)**, seeking forgiveness from those we have wronged **(Matthew 5:23-24)**, and extending forgiveness to those who have wronged us **(Ephesians 4:32).** Additionally, prayer is a powerful tool for practicing forgiveness, as it can help us release our anger and bitterness and open our hearts to forgiveness (**Matthew 6:9-15).** By practicing forgiveness, we can experience healing and transformation in our lives.

Worship and advocacy intersect in the healing process from the wounds of injustice trauma. Worship can provide a space for individuals and communities to connect with God and experience spiritual renewal, which can inspire and motivate advocacy **(Isaiah 58:6-7).**

Advocacy, on the other hand, can be an expression of worship by seeking to create a more just and equitable society in line with God's values **(Amos 5:24).** By bringing these two concepts together, individuals and communities can experience healing and transformation in both their spiritual and physical lives. Through worship and advocacy, we can work towards a world where justice, mercy, and love prevail (**Micah 6:8).**

Worship and spirituality can play a critical role in the process of healing from the wounds of injustice trauma. The Bible teaches that we can find comfort and strength through worship and prayer (**Psalm 34:18, Philippians 4:6-7**). In times of hardship and pain, we can turn to God and find solace in His presence.

Additionally, spirituality can provide a framework for understanding and processing our experiences of injustice trauma. Through worship and spiritual practices, we can seek to make sense of our pain and find meaning and purpose in our suffering.

(Romans 8:28). *And we know that all things work together for good to those who love God, to those who are the called according to His purpose*

Worship and advocacy are connected in their ability to create positive change in the world. The Bible teaches that true worship is demonstrated through acts of mercy, justice, and compassion towards others **(Isaiah 1:17, James 1:27)**. Advocacy seeks to address systemic issues of injustice and create a more equitable society, in line with God's values. Through the combination of worship and advocacy, individuals and communities can work towards creating a world where justice, love, and mercy prevail **(Micah 6:8).**

Injustice trauma refers to the emotional, psychological, and physical responses that people experience when they witness or are subjected to unjust or unfair treatment. It is a type of trauma that can result from various forms of discrimination, oppression, marginalization, and violence, such as racism, sexism, and the violation of the expression of religious freedoms. The effects of injustice trauma can be long-lasting and far-reaching, and they can vary from person to person.

Some common effects of injustice trauma include:

- Emotional distress: People who experience injustice trauma may feel anxious, angry, sad, frustrated, or helpless. They may struggle with feelings of shame, guilt, or self-doubt, and they may find it difficult to trust others.

- Physical symptoms: Injustice trauma can also manifest in physical symptoms such as headaches, fatigue, insomnia, gastrointestinal problems, and muscle tension.

- Behavioral changes: People who experience injustice trauma may change their behavior in response to the trauma, such as withdrawing from social activities, avoiding certain places or situations, or becoming more hypervigilant.

- Relationship difficulties: Injustice trauma can also impact relationships, leading to trust issues, conflicts, and a breakdown in communication.

- Self-esteem issues: People who experience injustice trauma may struggle with feelings of inadequacy or low self-worth, which can impact their ability to succeed in various areas of life.

It is important to note that injustice trauma is not limited to individuals who have personally experienced discrimination or oppression. Witnessing or hearing about injustice can also have a significant impact on mental health and well-being.

Happy Mother's Day Ladies! You Are Truly Special!

LIVING IN FAITH EVERYDAY

And the peace of God, which surpasses all understanding, will guard your hearts and your minds in Christ Jesus. And the peace of God, which transcends all understanding, will guard your hearts and your minds in Christ Jesus. Then you will experience God's peace, which exceeds anything we can understand.

- Philippians 4:7

List Five Prayers for Some One

1.

2.

3.

4.

5.

List 5 Prayers for Yourself

6.

7.

8.

9.

10.

Made in the USA
Middletown, DE
03 November 2023